Changing Your Name in Canada

Changing Your Name in Canada

Tanya Lee Howe & Eileen Velthuis

Self-Counsel Press
(a division of)
International Self-Counsel Press Ltd.
Canada   USA

Self-Counsel Press acknowledges the financial support of the Government of Canada through the Canada Book Fund for our publishing activities.

First edition: 2014

Library and Archives Canada Cataloguing in Publication

Howe, Tanya Lee, author

Changing your name in Canada / Tanya Lee Howe & Eileen Velthuis.

(Reference series)

Issued in print and electronic formats.

ISBN 978-1-77040-203-4 (pbk.).—ISBN 978-1-77040-948-4 (epub).—ISBN 978-1-77040-949-1 (kindle)

1. Names, Personal—Law and legislation—Canada. I. Velthuis, Eileen, author II. Title.

| KE501.H69 2014 | 346.7101'2 | C2014-901340-X |
| KF468.H69 2014 | | C2014-901341-8 |

MIX
Paper from
responsible sources
FSC® C004071

Self-Counsel Press
(a division of)
International Self-Counsel Press Ltd.

North Vancouver, BC
Canada

Contents

Notice to Readers

Laws are constantly changing. Every effort is made to keep this publication as current as possible. However, the author, the publisher, and the vendor of this book make no representations or warranties regarding the outcome or the use to which the information in this book is put and are not assuming any liability for any claims, losses, or damages arising out of the use of this book. The reader should not rely on the author or the publisher of this book for any professional advice. Please be sure that you have the most recent edition.

Note: The fees quoted in this book are correct at the date of publication. However, fees are subject to change without notice. For current fees, please check with the court registry or appropriate government office nearest you.

Prices, commissions, fees, and other costs mentioned in the text or shown in samples in this book probably do not reflect real costs where you live. Inflation and other factors, including geography, can cause the costs you might encounter to be much higher or even much lower than those we show. The dollar amounts shown are simply intended as representative examples.

Chapter 1

An Introduction to Changing Your Name in Canada

In the past, changing a surname is something most Canadian men never did, and most Canadian women would only do once or twice in their lives when they got married or divorced. Nowadays more men are opting to share their spouse's last name by combining the two names or even switching to a spouse's last name, many women still change their names upon marriage or divorce, and some people change their names for reasons that have nothing to do with marriage or divorce.

Although changing a name is a task infrequently done by any one individual, it can be quite involved. There are so many places, people, and organizations you need to contact when you want your name changed, and each one has its own ways to do it, and its own red tape and bureaucracy. At the end of the book, in Appendix II, you'll find an Identification Update List to help you contact everyone who needs to be alerted to your name change.

To complicate matters more, each province and territory has its own vital statistics agency rules and legal acts when it comes to formally or informally changing a name. A *formal* name change means a legal change to the first name, surname, or both in which the person's birth records are updated with the new name and a new birth certificate is issued. An *informal* name change usually means opting to use your spouse's surname when you get married, or switching back to a previous surname or birth name if you've recently divorced. An informal change does not affect your birth certificate.

People change their names for a variety of reasons, which may include the following:

- Marriage.
- Divorce.
- Correction of a typo or changing an odd spelling of a name.
- Dislike of the name that was given at birth.
- To remove problems with confusion or mispronunciations.
- To use a name the person is known for such as a nickname (e.g., the name is Robert but the person is only known as Bob).
- Protection from others, perhaps to prevent harassment by an individual.

Names are inherently personal, and as such, your reason for changing your name is your choice. Whatever your reason, this book will help you know what to do and in what order, depending on where you reside in the country, to change your name legally and across all of your identification and documentation.

Depending on where you currently reside, and where you were born, you may need to contact your former jurisdiction as well as your current one. This book discusses the procedures for every province and territory in Canada. The Resources section in Appendix I lists Vital Statistics contact information in other parts of the world.

This book discusses name changes for marriage, divorce, amendments to names, and how to change a child's name. It also includes the costs, which were current at the time of publication but are subject to change. Turn to the chapter for your province of residence for specific instructions.

Chapter 2

Alberta

It is a relatively simple process to apply for a formal, legal name change in Alberta. This chapter will provide you with the information you will need.

1. Who Doesn't Require a Legal Name Change?

Not everyone needs to go through the formal process to legally change his or her name in Alberta as you will see in the following four sections.

1.1 Marriage

If a person wants to take his or her spouse's name through marriage, the process is simple. Either spouse may choose to use the other's last name, or a combination of the two last names. You can combine the two last names using a hyphen or space. The order of the two names is up to you.

You will need to update all your identification (see Appendix II) by visiting with or sending the official marriage certificate (or a notarized copy of it) to the various places you want your name changed (e.g., credit card companies, Social Insurance). Organizations may have additional requirements, so you will have to contact them to find out if you'll need to send more than a marriage certificate.

1.2 Divorce

If you're recently divorced, you can return to the last name you had before marriage. You will follow the same process as you did when you got married by contacting the various organizations (e.g., banks, credit card companies) and asking what they need in order to change your identification. Many places will need to see your official divorce certificate (or a notarized copy of it) and your birth certificate.

1.3 Change of parent

You can add or delete the father or co-parent from the birth record of a child who is younger than 12 years old; at that time, the child's name may be changed. The child has to be born in Alberta to do this.

Both parents can apply to add a father or co-parent by completing a Joint Application.

If a father or co-parent is being deleted from the Registration of Birth, a parentage declaration order is needed in order to amend the parentage. Contact Service Alberta for more about this (see section **6.**)

1.4 Amendment of a name

In some circumstances, a person can correct his or her name without completing the legal name change process. At the time of birth, registration is completed and filed permanently with Vital Statistics. If the registration includes incomplete, missing, or incorrect information, you can request to correct it.

If you were not born in Alberta, you will need to contact the Vital Statistics or similar agency in the jurisdiction where you were born.

You can contact a registry agent in your area or contact Vital Statistics directly for an amendment. You can complete the Request to Amend an Alberta Vital Statistics Registration form online (www.servicealberta.ca/pdf/vs/Amendment_Form_2013. pdf). Vital Statistics will contact you with instructions of what to do next such as submitting affidavits and evidence (if necessary).

The fee is $20 unless the amendment is made within 90 days of the birth or event that necessitated the amendment.

2. Who Is Eligible to Apply?

The following outlines who is eligible to apply for a formal name change:

- A resident of Alberta.
- Someone who is 18 years of age or older.
- You can apply for a name change if it is your own name.
- You can change your spouse's name (you'll need a marriage certificate and his or her consent).
- You can change a partner's name (you'll need a Statutory Declaration of Adult Interdependent Relationship, which is for same-sex or common-law couples, as well as the person's consent).
- You can change a child's name (you'll need a birth certificate showing parentage; and the child must be younger than 18 and give his or her consent).
- You can change a ward's name (you'll need a copy of the guardianship order; and the child must be younger than 18 and give his or her consent if 12 or over).

If you're younger than the age of 18, you may still change your name if one or more of the following applies:

- You're legally married.
- You're living in an adult interdependent relationship.
- You're the parent of a child.
- You're the guardian of a child.

If you are a temporary resident (e.g., work or student visa), or tourist/visitor, you cannot apply for a name change in Alberta.

3. Name Restrictions

There are some restrictions on what type of name you can choose:

- You must include a first and last name.
- The name has to use the Roman alphabet.

- The name cannot have non-letter characters (i.e., no symbols).
- The name cannot include profanity.
- The name cannot include numbers.

Some punctuation marks are acceptable, such as a period, a hyphen, and an apostrophe. If you want to have an accent in your name, you will need to contact the registry to find out which accents are acceptable. There is also a limit to the amount of punctuation marks and accents that will be accepted.

4. Application Process

You cannot apply online for a legal name change in Alberta. You have to physically go to a registry and pick up the booklet of forms. When you are done completing the forms, you have to return to the registry to submit the forms to a registry agent. The registry has strict rules on how to complete the forms; for example, the forms come in a booklet and if you remove any of the forms from it, you will have to begin the application process all over again with a new booklet. Keep in mind, the perforated pages in the booklet tear easily so be careful when completing the forms. You can see an example of this form in the download kit included with this book.

4.1 Necessary documents

You will need to bring your original Canadian birth certificate. If you don't have the original, you can get a notarized copy of your Canadian birth certificate. If you were born in Alberta, and you don't have an original birth certificate, Vital Statistics will find the original on file for you. You're required to include with the application all original birth certificates.

People who were not born in Alberta will need to contact their former jurisdiction where they were born. That jurisdiction may have different instructions for applying for a new birth certificate with the new, formally changed name.

You will need to provide the registry agent with a proof of identity document when you are submitting your name change application. These are the requirements:

- Issued by a government body (e.g., driver's licence, Permanent Resident Card, Canadian citizenship certificate, treaty status card).
- Must include the person's full name.
- Must include the person's photo.
- Contains a distinct identification number.
- Must be valid (i.e., not expired).
- Must be a document that has been issued within the last five years.

Each situation is different, but you also may be required to provide the following:

- Marriage certificates (original certificates and not the civil or religious marriage certificates).
- Written consents (if you are changing the name of a child, partner, or spouse).
- Dispensations .
- Affidavit.
- Proof of marital status.
- Court order.
- Guardianship order.
- Affidavit of Sole Guardianship.
- Notarized translation of documents (including an affidavit affirmed or sworn by a translator).

Those born outside of Canada will need a Canadian citizenship certificate or Permanent Resident Card. The registry will not accept the following documents from those born outside Canada:

- Social insurance card.
- Notice of birth registration.
- Baptismal certificate.
- Immigration documents.
- Passport.
- Driver's licence.

- Commemoration of Canadian citizenship.
- Health-care card.

If you have previously had a legal name change, you must disclose this information. You will also need a copy of all your previous Change of Name Certificates. However, if you have completed the previous change of name in Alberta, Vital Statistics will have access to this in its records. This doesn't include changing a name by marriage or from a legal adoption order. You can see an example of this form in the download kit included with this book.

4.2 Fingerprint requirements

The Alberta RCMP requires a person who is completing a legal name change to provide fingerprints as part of his or her application process. This applies to all persons who are 12 years of age or older. The fingerprints are cross-referenced with criminal records by the Canadian Criminal Real Time Identification Service (CCRTIS) in Ottawa. Note that the fingerprints are not kept on file with the RCMP, CCRTIS, or Vital Statistics after the application process is complete.

You can contact the local RCMP to take your fingerprints, either manually (i.e., on paper) or electronically. If manual fingerprints are taken, you'll need to include the original form when you submit your change of name application. Electronic fingerprints are submitted by the RCMP to the CCRTIS, and you'll receive a confirmation letter from CCRTIS, which you will submit with your change of name application.

4.3 Publication of name change

The change of name booklet includes a form you'll need to sign in regards to publication of the name change. According to the *Vital Statistics Act*, all registered name changes must be published in the *Alberta Gazette* in both the online and paper formats. See the example in the download kit included with this book.

If there is a reason you don't want your new name published (e.g., due to someone stalking you or violent domestic situations), you can put forth an order to the Court of Queen's Bench dispensing with publication. You will need to include the court order with your change of name application. Note that it is very rare that the court will dispense with the publication requirements.

4.4 Affidavit

In the booklet for the change of name application, you will find an affidavit, in which you will need to swear or affirm that what you said in your application is true. Without removing it from the booklet, you will need to take it to a Commissioner for Oaths or a notary public in Alberta to have it properly sworn or affirmed. See Sample 7.

You can find a commissioner or notary either in the local court house, or look in the Yellow Pages for an independent notary service. There is a fee for this service, which can vary, so shop around to find the most reasonable price.

5. Cost and Payment Methods

The government fee is $120 per application (including either one person or an entire family); however, there is also the fee the independent registry charges on top of the government fee. In some cases, it may be as high as, or even higher than $300 (including the government fee). The registry fee has not been capped by the government, so make sure you do some research to find the best price.

You can pay the registry by cash, debit card, credit card, money order, or traveller's cheque. If you pay using a personal cheque, the application is delayed for 14 days in order to process the cheque.

There is also an additional cost of $25 for the RCMP fingerprint processing fee. Note that this fee varies depending on your jurisdiction.

The swearing or affirming of the affidavit by a commissioner or notary will also have a fee, which can vary so shop around.

6. Contact

On the Service Alberta website, there is a list of independent registries that provide services for Vital Statistics. You can also find them listed in the Yellow Pages under "licensing services."

Note: You must be physically present in a registry office; you cannot send your information in the mail. It has to be submitted by a registry agent.

If you have questions, you can talk to your local registry, or you can contact Service Alberta.

Website: www.servicealberta.gov.ab.ca/1641.cfm

Telephone: 780-427-7013 (Edmonton and surrounding areas)
Toll Free: 310-0000 then dial 780-427-7013

Mail:
Service Alberta
Vital Statistics
Box 2023
Edmonton, Alberta T5J 4W7

Chapter 3

British Columbia

It is a relatively simple process to apply for a formal, legal name change in British Columbia. This chapter will provide you with the information you will need.

1. Who Doesn't Require a Legal Name Change?

Not everyone needs to go through the formal process to legally change his or her name in British Columbia as you will see in the following sections.

1.1 Marriage

If a person wants to take his or her spouse's name through marriage, the process is simple. Either spouse may choose to use the other's last name, or a combination of the two last names. You can combine the two last names using a hyphen or space. The order of the two names is up to you.

You will need to update all your identification (see Appendix II) by visiting with or sending the official marriage certificate (or a notarized copy of it) to various places (e.g., credit card companies, Social Insurance). Organizations may have additional requirements, so you will have to contact them to find out if you need to send more than a marriage certificate.

1.2 Divorce

If you're recently divorced, you can return to the last name you had before marriage. You will follow the same process as you did when you got married by contacting the various organizations (e.g., banks, credit card companies) and asking what they need in order to change your identification. Many places will need to see the official divorce certificate (or a notarized copy of it) and your birth certificate.

1.3 Amendment of a name

In some circumstances, a person can correct his or her name without completing the legal name change process. At the time of birth, registration is completed and filed permanently with Vital Statistics. If the registration includes incomplete, missing, or incorrect information, you can request to correct it.

If you were not born in British Columbia, you will need to contact Vital Statistics or a similar agency in the jurisdiction where you were born.

You can contact a registry agent in your area or contact Vital Statistics directly for an amendment. You can also complete the Statutory Declaration Re: Correction of Error or Omission in Birth Registration form online (www.vs.gov.bc.ca/forms/vsa412B_fill. pdf).

The fee is $27 at time of writing.

See the download kit included with this book.

2. Who Is Eligible to Apply?

The following outlines who is eligible to apply for a formal name change in British Columbia:

- A resident of British Columbia for at least the previous three months.
- Someone who is 19 years of age or older.
- You can apply for a name change if it is your own name.

- You can apply to change a child's name (you'll need a birth certificate showing parentage; and the child must be younger than 19, but if older than 12 must also give his or her consent. Your spouse's or the other parent's consent may also be needed.)

If you're younger than the age of 19, you may still change your name if one or more of the following applies:

- You're legally married.
- You're living in an adult interdependent relationship.
- You're the parent or guardian of a child.

If you are a temporary resident (e.g., have a work or student visa), or are a tourist/visitor, you cannot apply for a name change in British Columbia.

3. Name Restrictions

There are some restrictions on what type of name you can choose:

- You must include a first and last name.
- The name has to use the Roman alphabet.
- The name cannot have non-letter characters (i.e., no symbols).
- The name cannot include profanity.
- The name cannot include numbers.

Some punctuation marks are acceptable, such as a period, a hyphen, and an apostrophe. If you want to have an accent in your name, you will need to contact the registry to find out what accents are acceptable. There is also a limit to the amount of punctuation marks and accents that will be accepted.

4. Application Process

You can get the current Application for Change of Name form from Vital Statistics or Service BC offices or on Vital Statistics' website at www.vs.gov.bc.ca/forms/vsa529.pdf; you also need to separately obtain a fingerprinting package (see section 4.2). Follow the instructions in the packages carefully.

When you are done completing the Application form, you have to return to the registry to submit the form to a registry agent in person. The fingerprinting package will be submitted by the RCMP; it will not be returned to you.

It can take a minimum of four to six weeks to process your application (longer if information needs clarification).

Refer to the download kit included with this book for an example of an Application form.

4.1 Necessary documents

You will need to bring your original Canadian birth certificate. If you don't have the original, bring a notarized copy of your Canadian birth certificate. If you were born in British Columbia, and you don't have an original birth certificate, Vital Statistics will find the original on file for you. You must include with the application all original birth certificates.

People who were not born in British Columbia will have to contact their former jurisdiction where they were born. That jurisdiction may have different instructions for applying for a new birth certificate with the new name. If born outside of Canada, certified copies of immigration papers or a permanent resident card is required.

A marriage certificate may be necessary, as well as proof of custody if a parent is applying to change a child's name without the other parent's consent.

You will need to provide the registry agent with a proof of your foundation identity, with your identification meeting the following criteria:

- Original British Columbia birth certificates or notarized copies.

- Any Canadian immigration identity documentation such as Canadian citizenship certificate or Permanent Resident Card, or certified copies.

Applicants must include the following:

- Original marriage certificates (original certificates and not the civil or religious marriage certificates, if married in Canada).

- A photocopy of marriage certificates if married outside of Canada.

- Written consents (if you are changing the name of a child, partner, or spouse; these are included for you to fill out as part of the Application form)

If you have previously had a legal name change, you must disclose this information by also including any original Change of Name certificates in former names.

4.2 Fingerprint requirements

The RCMP requires a person who is completing a legal name change to provide fingerprints as part of his or her application process. This applies to all persons who are 18 years of age or older. The fingerprints are cross-referenced with criminal records by the Canadian Criminal Real Time Identification Service (CCRTIS) in Ottawa. Note that the fingerprints are not kept on file with the RCMP, CCRTIS, or Vital Statistics after the application process is complete.

Once you decide to apply to legally change your name, obtain a fingerprint package, either in person at Vital Statistics or Service BC, by phoning 250-952-2681, or by emailing HLTH.CNFORMS@ gov.bc.ca.

4.3 Publication of name change

After a certificate of change of name is issued, the chief executive officer must publish the person's new and former names, date of birth, municipality of residence, and effective date, unless the person is a minor whose name is being changed to that of the adult applicant or if the chief executive officer decides publication is not in the public interest. This information used to be printed in the *BC Gazette* but now is fully searchable online at www.qplegaleze.ca.

4.4 Statutory declaration

As part of the change of name application form, you will find a statutory declaration, in which you will need to swear or affirm that what you said in your application is true. You will need to take it to a lawyer, notary public, or commissioner for taking affidavits in British Columbia to have it properly sworn or affirmed.

You can find a commissioner, lawyer, or notary either through the local courthouse or in the Yellow Pages. There is a fee for this service, which can vary, so shop around to find the most reasonable price.

5. Cost and Payment Methods

The government fee is currently $137 per application (or one legal name change and one large certificate); for additional individuals younger than 19 years old on the adult's application add $27 each. Also add $25 per person for criminal record checks levied on behalf of the RCMP, and bear in mind that local police departments may charge a fingerprinting fee which can vary.

You can pay the registry by certified cheque or money order payable to the Minister of Finance, or by credit card.

The swearing or affirming of the affidavit by a commissioner or notary will have a fee, which can vary so shop around; Vital Statistics currently charges $17 for document witnessing.

6. Contact

If you have questions, you can contact the British Columbia Vital Statistics Agency.

Website: www.vs.gov.bc.ca

Telephone: 604-660-2937 or 250-952-2681
Toll free: 1-888-876-1633

Mail:
British Columbia Vital Statistics Agency
PO Box 9657 STN PROV GOVT
Victoria, BC V8W 9P3

Chapter 4

Manitoba

It is a relatively simple process to apply for a formal, legal name change in Manitoba. This chapter will provide you with the information you will need.

1. Who Doesn't Require a Legal Name Change?

Not everyone needs to go through the formal process to legally change his or her name in Manitoba as you will see in the following sections.

1.1 Marriage

If a person wants to take his or her spouse's name through marriage, the process is simple. Either spouse may choose to retain his or her last name; use the other's last name; combine last names, in either order, with or without a hyphen; or assume his or her partner's last name and retain his or her surname as a given, middle name.

In order to update all your identification (see Appendix II), show your official marriage certificate (or notarized copy) and government-issued identification to the various places you'll want your name changed (e.g., credit card companies, Social Insurance).

Organizations may be different, so you will have to contact them to find out if there are any special requirements.

1.2 Divorce

If you're recently divorced, you can return to the last name you had before marriage. You will follow the same process as you did when you got married by contacting various organizations (e.g., banks, credit card companies) and asking what they need in order to change your identification. Many places will need to see your official divorce certificate (or a notarized copy of it) and your birth certificate.

1.3 Amendment of a name

In some circumstances, a person can correct his or her name without completing the legal name change process. At the time of birth, registration is completed and filed permanently with Vital Statistics. If the registration includes incomplete, missing, or incorrect information, you can request to correct it.

If you were not born in Manitoba, you will need to contact Vital Statistics or the similar agency in the jurisdiction where you were born.

You can contact a registry agent in your area or contact Vital Statistics directly for an amendment.

2. Who Is Eligible to Apply?

The following outlines who is eligible to apply for a formal name change in Manitoba:

- A resident of Manitoba for at least the past three months.

- Someone who is 18 years of age or older; has been married; has cohabited in a common-law relationship; or is a parent with custody of the child and he or she wants to change the name of his or her child.

- You can apply for a name change if it is your own name.

- You can apply to change a child's name (you'll need a birth certificate showing parentage; you need to have custody or written consent from the custodial parent; and the child must be younger than 18 and give his or her consent if he or she is 12 or older).

3. Name Restrictions

There are some restrictions on what type of name you can choose:

- You must include a first and last name.
- The name has to use the Roman alphabet.
- The name cannot have non-letter characters (i.e., no symbols).
- The name cannot include profanity.
- The name cannot include numbers.

Some punctuation marks are acceptable such as a period, a hyphen, and apostrophe. If you want to have an accent in your name, you will need to contact the registry to find out what accents are acceptable. There is also a limit to the amount of punctuation marks and accents that will be accepted.

4. Application Process

You cannot currently apply online for a legal name change in Manitoba. You have to contact a registry and ask for the forms. When you are done completing the forms, you have to return the forms to a registry agent.

Once you have received your change of name, make sure to contact every organization on the Identification Update List (Appendix II) and on the list of Manitoba Government Contacts (see download kit included with this book).

4.1 Necessary documents

You will need to bring your original Canadian birth certificate. If you don't have the original, you can use a notarized copy of your Canadian birth certificate. If you were born in Manitoba, and you don't have an original birth certificate, Vital Statistics will find the original on file for you.

You're required to include with the application all original birth certificates.

People not born in Manitoba will have to contact their former jurisdiction where they were born. That jurisdiction may have different instructions for applying for a new birth certificate with the new name.

You will need to provide the registry agent with a proof of identity document when you are submitting your name change application. These are the requirements:

- Issued by a government body (e.g., driver's licence, Permanent Resident Card, Canadian citizenship certificate, Status card).
- Must include the person's full name.
- Must include the person's photo.
- Contains a distinct identification number.
- Must be valid (i.e., not expired).
- Must be a document that has been issued within the last five years.

Each situation is different, but you also may be required to provide the following:

- Marriage certificates (original certificates and not the civil or religious marriage certificates).
- Written consents (if you are changing the name of a child, partner, or spouse).
- Dispensations.
- Affidavit.
- Proof of marital status.
- Court order.
- Guardianship order.
- Affidavit of Sole Guardianship.
- Notarized translation of documents (including an affidavit affirmed or sworn by a translator).

For those born outside of Canada, you will need a Canadian citizenship certificate or Permanent Resident Card. The registry will not accept the following documents from those born outside Canada:

- Social insurance card.
- Notice of birth registration.
- Baptismal certificate.
- Immigration documents.
- Passport.
- Driver's licence.
- Commemoration of Canadian citizenship.
- Health-care card.

If you have previously had a legal name change, you must disclose this information. You will also need a copy of all your previous Change of Name Certificates. However, if you have completed the previous change of name in Manitoba, Vital Statistics will have access to this in its records.

4.2 Fingerprint requirements

The RCMP requires a person who is completing a legal name change to provide fingerprints as part of his or her application process. This applies to all persons who are 12 years of age or older. The fingerprints are cross-referenced with criminal records by the Canadian Criminal Real Time Identification Service (CCRTIS) in Ottawa. Note that the fingerprints are not kept on file with the RCMP, CCRTIS, or Vital Statistics after the application process is complete.

You can contact your local RCMP to take your fingerprints, either manually (i.e., on paper) or electronically. For manual fingerprints, you'll need to include the originals when you submit your change of name application. Electronic fingerprints are submitted by the RCMP to the CCRTIS, and you'll receive a confirmation letter from CCRTIS, which you will submit with your change of name application.

Contact Vital Statistics first for the change of name forms and follow the instructions.

4.3 Publication of name change

According to law, all registered name changes must be published in the *Manitoba Gazette* once approved.

If there is a reason you don't want your new name published (e.g., due to someone stalking you or violent domestic situations), you can ask to dispense with publication (ask Vital Statistics for information on how to do this). Note that it is very rare that the court will dispense with the publication requirements.

4.4 Affidavit

As part of your change of name application, you will find a section called Affidavit of Qualification and Bona Fides, in which you will need to swear or affirm that what you said in your application is true. You will need to take it to a Commissioner for Oaths or a lawyer or notary public in Manitoba to have it properly sworn or affirmed.

You can find a commissioner, lawyer, or notary either in the local court house or in the Yellow Pages. There is a fee for this service, which can vary, so shop around to find the most reasonable price.

5. Cost and Payment Methods

The government fee for a legal change of name including the *Manitoba Gazette* fee is $130.88; for each additional family member included in the same application, add $50.00. You can pay the registry by cash or debit card (if at the registry in person), or by credit card, money order, or cheque.

There is an additional RCMP fingerprint processing fee. Note that this fee varies depending on your jurisdiction.

The swearing or affirming of the affidavit by a commissioner, lawyer, or notary will also have a fee, which can vary, so shop around.

6. Contact

If you have questions, you can talk to your local registry, or you can contact Vital Statistics:

Website: vitalstats.gov.mb.ca

Telephone: 204-945-3701
Telephone toll free within Canada: 1-866-949-9296
Fax: 204-948-3128

Mail:
Vital Statistics Agency
254 Portage Avenue
Winnipeg, MB R3C 0B6

Chapter 5

New Brunswick

It is a relatively simple process to apply for a formal, legal name change in New Brunswick. This chapter will provide you with the information you will need.

1. Who Doesn't Require a Legal Name Change?

Not everyone needs to go through the formal process to legally change his or name in New Brunswick as you will see in the following sections.

1.1 Marriage

If a person wants to take his or her spouse's name through marriage, the process is simple. Either spouse may choose to retain his or her last name; use the other's last name; combine last names, in either order, with or without a hyphen; or assume a partner's last name and retain his or her surname as a given, middle name.

In order to update all your identification (see Appendix II), show your official marriage certificate and government-issued identification to the various places you'll want your name changed (e.g., credit card companies, Social Insurance). Organizations may be different, so you will have to contact them to find out if there are any special requirements.

1.2 Divorce

If you're recently divorced, you can return to the last name you had before marriage. You will follow the same process as you did when you got married by contacting various organizations (e.g., banks, credit card companies) and asking what they need in order to change your identification. Many places will need to see the official divorce certificate (or a notarized copy of it) and your birth certificate.

1.3 Amendment of a name

In some circumstances, a person can correct his or her name without completing the legal name change process. At the time of birth, registration is completed and filed permanently with Vital Statistics. If the registration includes incomplete, missing, or incorrect information, you can request to correct it.

If you were not born in New Brunswick, you will need to contact Vital Statistics or a similar agency in the jurisdiction where you were born.

2. Who Is Eligible to Apply?

The following outlines who is eligible to apply for a formal name change:

- A resident of New Brunswick (for at least the previous three months).
- Someone who is 19 years of age or older; is or has been married; or is a parent with lawful custody of the child whose name he or she is applying to change.
- You can apply for a name change if it is your own name.
- You can apply to change a child's name (you'll need custody and a birth certificate showing parentage; and the child must be younger than 19 and give his or her consent if 12 or older).

3. Name Restrictions

There are some restrictions on what type of name you can choose:

- You must include a first and last name.
- The name has to use the Roman alphabet.
- The name cannot have non-letter characters (i.e., no symbols).
- The name cannot include profanity.
- The name cannot include numbers.

Some punctuation marks are acceptable, such as a period, a hyphen, and an apostrophe. If you want to have an accent in your name, you will need to contact the registry to find out what accents are acceptable. There is also a limit to the amount of punctuation marks and accents that will be accepted.

4. Application Process

You cannot apply online for a legal name change in New Brunswick. You have to physically go to a registry and pick up the information package and application, or have it mailed to you. When you are done completing the forms, you have to return it to the registry.

4.1 Necessary documents

You will need to have your original Canadian birth certificate. If you don't have the original, you can get a notarized copy of your Canadian birth certificate. If you were born in New Brunswick, and you don't have an original birth certificate, Vital Statistics will find the original on file for you. You're required to include with the application all original birth certificates.

People who were not born in New Brunswick will have to contact their former jurisdiction where they were born. That jurisdiction may have different instructions for applying for a new birth certificate with the new name.

You will need to provide the registry agent with a proof of identity document when you are submitting your name change application. These are the requirements:

- Issued by a government body (e.g., driver's licence, Permanent Resident Card, Canadian citizenship certificate, Status card).
- Must include the person's full name.

- Must include the person's photo.
- Contains a distinct identification number.
- Must be valid (i.e., not expired).
- Must be a document that has been issued within the last five years.

Each situation is different, but you also may be required to provide the following:

- Marriage certificates (original certificates and not the civil or religious marriage certificates).
- Written consents (if you are changing the name of a child, partner, or spouse).
- Dispensations .
- Affidavit.
- Proof of marital status.
- Court order.
- Guardianship order.
- Affidavit of Sole Guardianship.
- Notarized translation of documents (including an affidavit affirmed or sworn by a translator).

For those born outside of Canada, you will need a Canadian citizenship certificate or Permanent Residency Card. The registry will not accept the following documents from those born outside Canada:

- Social insurance card.
- Notice of birth registration.
- Baptismal certificate.
- Immigration documents.
- Passport.
- Driver's licence.
- Commemoration of Canadian citizenship.
- Health-care card.

If you have previously had a legal name change, or have a criminal record, you must disclose this information. You will also need a copy of all your previous Change of Name Certificates.

4.2 Publication of name change

According to the *Vital Statistics Act*, all registered name changes must be published in *The Royal Gazette* by the Registrar.

If there is a reason you don't want your new name published (e.g., due to someone stalking you or violent domestic situations), you can put forth an order to the Court of Queen's Bench dispensing with publication. You will need to include the court order with your change of name application. Note that it is very rare that the court will dispense with the publication requirements.

4.3 Statements

You will need to find a sponsor; that is, you will need someone to declare that he or she has known you for at least two years and can verify your identity.

As part of your change of name application, you will also need to swear or affirm that what you said in your application is true. You will need to take your application to a Commissioner for Oaths, a lawyer, or a notary public in New Brunswick to have it properly sworn or affirmed.

You can find a commissioner, lawyer, or notary either in the local court house or in the Yellow Pages. There is a fee for this service, which can vary, so shop around to find the most reasonable price.

5. Cost and Payment Methods

The government fees are currently (not including HST):

- $100 to change a given name.
- $125 to change a surname.
- $50 to change a child's surname at the same time as a parent's surname is changed.
- $15 for a duplicate change of name certificate.
- $15 for a name change search.

You can pay the registry by cheque or money order payable to Service New Brunswick, or by Visa, MasterCard, or American Express.

The swearing or affirming of the affidavit by a commissioner or notary will have a fee, which can vary so shop around.

6. Contact

If you have questions, you can talk to your local registry, or you can contact Service New Brunswick:

Websites:

www.snb.ca/e/1000/1000-01/e/index-e.asp

www2.gnb.ca/content/gnb/en/services/services_
renderer.17476.Change_of_Name.html

Telephone: 506-453-2385
Toll free: 1-888-762-8600
Fax: 506-444-4139

Mail:
Vital Statistics
Service New Brunswick
PO Box 1998
Fredericton, NB E3B 5G4

Chapter 6

Newfoundland and Labrador

It is a relatively simple process to apply for a formal, legal name change in Newfoundland and Labrador. This chapter will provide you with the information you will need.

1. Who Doesn't Require a Legal Name Change?

Not everyone needs to go through the formal process to legally change his or her name in Newfoundland and Labrador as you will see in the following sections.

1.1 Marriage

If a person wants to take his or her spouse's name through marriage, the process is simple. Either spouse may choose to use the other's last name, or a combination of the two last names. You can combine the two last names using a hyphen or space. The order of the two names is up to you.

You will need to update all your identification (see Appendix II) by showing your official marriage certificate (or a notarized copy of it) to the various places you"ll want your name changed (e.g., credit card companies, Social Insurance). Organizations may have additional requirements, so you will have to contact them to find out if you'll need to show more than a marriage certificate.

1.2 Divorce

If you're recently divorced, you can return to the last name you had before marriage. You will follow the same process as you did when you got married by contacting various organizations (e.g., banks, credit card companies) and asking what they need in order to change your identification. Many places will need to see your official divorce certificate (or a notarized copy of it) and your birth certificate.

1.3 Amendment of a name

In some circumstances, a person can correct his or her name without completing the legal name change process. At the time of birth, registration is completed and filed permanently with Service NL. If the registration includes incomplete, missing, or incorrect information, you can request to correct it.

If you were not born in Newfoundland and Labrador, you will need to contact the Vital Statistics or a similar agency in the jurisdiction where you were born.

2. Who Is Eligible to Apply?

The following outlines who is eligible to apply for a formal name change:

- A resident of Newfoundland and Labrador for at least the previous three months.
- Someone who is 19 years of age or older; or is married; divorced; widowed; or the parent or guardian of a child.
- You can apply for a name change if it is your own name.
- You can apply to change a child's name (you'll need a birth certificate showing parentage; and the child must be younger than 19 and give his or her consent if 12 or older).

If you are a temporary resident (e.g., work or student visa), or tourist/visitor, you cannot apply for a name change in Newfoundland and Labrador.

3. Name Restrictions

There are some restrictions on what type of name you can choose:

- You must include a first and last name.
- The name has to use the Roman alphabet.
- The name cannot have non-letter characters (i.e., no symbols).
- The name cannot include profanity.
- The name cannot include numbers.

Some punctuation marks are acceptable, such as a period, a hyphen, and an apostrophe. If you want to have an accent in your name, you will need to contact the registry to find out what accents are acceptable. There is also a limit to the amount of punctuation marks and accents that will be accepted.

4. Application Process

You cannot apply online for a legal name change in Newfoundland and Labrador. You have to physically go to a registry and pick up the forms, or contact them to have them sent to you. When you are done completing the forms, you have to return them to the registry per the instructions on the forms.

See the download kit included with this book for an example of a form for an adult name change (Application for Change of Name of an Adult) and a sample application for a name change for a child (Application for Change of Name of a Child).

4.1 Necessary documents

You will need to bring your original Canadian birth certificate. If you don't have the original, you can get a notarized copy of your Canadian birth certificate. If you were born in Newfoundland and Labrador, and you don't have an original birth certificate, Vital Statistics will find the original on file for you. You're required to include with the application all original birth certificates.

People who were not born in Newfoundland and Labrador will have to contact their former jurisdiction where they were born to obtain a birth certificate.

A baptism certificate is an acceptable substitute only for those who were born in Newfoundland and Labrador who do not have a birth certificate.

You will need to provide the registry agent with a proof of identity document when you are submitting your name change application. These are the requirements:

- Issued by a government body (e.g., driver's licence, Permanent Resident Card, Canadian citizenship certificate, Status card).
- Must include the person's full name.
- Must include the person's photo.
- Contains a distinct identification number.
- Must be valid (i.e., not expired).
- Must be a document that has been issued within the last five years.

Each situation is different, but you also may be required to provide the following:

- Marriage certificates (original certificates and not the civil or religious marriage certificates).
- Written consents (if you are changing the name of a child, partner, or spouse).
- Dispensations.
- Affidavit.
- Proof of marital status.
- Court order.
- Guardianship order.
- Affidavit of Sole Guardianship.
- Notarized translation of documents (including an affidavit affirmed or sworn by a translator).

For those born outside of Canada, you will need a Canadian citizenship certificate or Permanent Resident Card. The registry will not accept the following documents from those born outside Canada:

- Social insurance card.
- Notice of birth registration.
- Baptismal certificate.
- Immigration documents.
- Passport.
- Driver's licence.
- Commemoration of Canadian citizenship.
- Health-care card.

If you have previously had a legal name change, you must disclose this information. You will also need a copy of all your previous Change of Name Certificates. However, if you have completed the previous change of name in Newfoundland and Labrador, Vital Statistics will have access to this in its records. This doesn't include changing a name by marriage or from a legal adoption order.

4.3 Publication of name change

The change of name form includes a section you'll need to sign in regards to publication of the name change. According to the law, all registered name changes must be published in the *Newfoundland and Labrador Gazette*.

If there is a reason you don't want your new name published (e.g., due to someone stalking you or violent domestic situations), you can request dispensing with publication. Ask Vital Statistics for information on how to request this. Note that it is very rare that the court will dispense with the publication requirements.

4.4 Affidavit

As part of the change of name application, you will find an affidavit, in which you will need to swear or affirm that what you said in your application is true. You will need to take it to a Commissioner for Oaths, a lawyer, or a notary public in Newfoundland and Labrador to have it properly sworn or affirmed.

You can find a commissioner, lawyer, or notary either through the local court house or in the Yellow Pages. There is a fee for this service, which can vary, so shop around to find the most reasonable price.

5. Cost and Payment Methods

The government fees are currently as follows:

- Change of surname: $45 ($25 for change of name and $20 for a new birth certificate, if you were born in the province).

- Change of given name: $45 ($25 for the change of name and $20 for a new birth certificate, if you were born in the province).

You can pay the registry by cash or debit card (in person), credit card, money order, or traveller's cheque. If you pay using a personal cheque, the application will be delayed for 14 days in order to process the cheque.

The swearing or affirming of the affidavit by a commissioner or notary will also have a fee, which can vary, so shop around.

6. Contact

If you have questions, you can talk to your local registry, or you can contact Service NL:

Website:

www.servicenl.gov.nl.ca/department/branches/divisions/vs.html

Telephone: 709-729-3308
Fax: 709-729-0946

Mail:
Service NL
Vital Statistics Division
Department of Government Services
PO Box 8700
St. John's NL A1B 4J6

Chapter 7

Northwest Territories

It is a relatively simple process to apply for a formal, legal name change in the Northwest Territories. This chapter will provide you with the information you will need.

1. Who Doesn't Require a Legal Name Change?

Not everyone needs to go through the formal process to legally change his or her name in the Northwest Territories as you will see in the following sections.

1.1 Marriage

If a person wants to take his or her spouse's name through marriage, the process is simple. Either spouse may choose to use the other's last name, or a combination of the two last names. You can combine the two last names using a hyphen or space. The order of the two names is up to you.

You will need to update all your identification (see Appendix II) by sending the official marriage certificate (or a notarized copy of it) to the various places you want your name changed (e.g., credit card companies, Social Insurance). Organizations may have

additional requirements, so you will have to contact them to find out if you'll need to send more than a marriage certificate.

1.2 Divorce or separation from common-law spouse

If you're recently divorced, you can return to the last surname you had before marriage or the name you were given at birth. You will follow the same process as you did when you got married by contacting various organizations (e.g., banks, credit card companies) and asking what they need in order to change your identification. Many places will need to see the official divorce certificate (or a notarized copy of it) and your birth certificate.

If you want to return to your former surname after separation, but you are not yet divorced or you were in a common-law relationship, you will need to submit a Statutory Declaration: Breakdown of Spousal Relationship.

The form can be found by using the following link: www.hss. gov.nt.ca/sites/default/files/statutory_declaration_breakdown_ of_spousal_relationship.pdf. An example can also be seen in the download kit included with this book.

2. Who Is Eligible to Apply?

The following outlines who is eligible to apply for a formal name change:

- A resident of the Northwest Territories (i.e., you have lived in the NWT at least 3 consecutive months in the 12-month period preceding the change of name application).

- A Canadian citizen.

- A permanent resident.

- A person who has reached the age of majority (19 years old or older).

If you're younger than 19, you can still apply for a change of name if you —

- have been a spouse,

- are currently a spouse, or

- have lawful custody of a child.

For those who are in a common-law relationship who would like to use their spouse's last name, they can complete a Statutory Declaration: Use of Common-Law Spouse's Last Name. You can find the form online by using the following link: www.hss. gov.nt.ca/sites/default/files/statutory_declaration_use_of_common_law_spouses_last_name.pdf. An example can also be seen in the download kit included with this book.

3. Name Restrictions

There are some restrictions on what type of name you can choose:

- The name must include a first name and surname.
- The surname cannot have more than two components (although surname can be joined by a hyphen).
- The name must use only the Roman alphabet.
- The name cannot cause confusion or embarrassment to another person.
- The name cannot be used in a manner to defraud or mislead the public.

If you want any type of punctuation (e.g., period, apostrophe, accent), you'll need to contact your local registry or Vital Statistics to find out what types are accepted. There may be a limit on the amount of punctuation in your name as well.

4. Change of Name of a Child

To change the name of a child, that child must be in your lawful custody. You cannot apply to have a child's name changed if there is a court order, parental agreement, or separation agreement that states the child's name cannot be changed.

If the other parent (or guardian) has lawful custody or access to the child, he or she will need to give his or her written consent in order for you to change the child's name. If the child is 12 years of age or older, you must have the child's written consent. Examples of the forms for this can be seen in the download kit included with this book, or at www.hss.gov.nt.ca/sites/default/files/application_for_change_of_name_package.pdf.

If your current spouse is not the biological parent of the child, but you want to change the child's last name to your current spouse's, you'll need the written consent of your spouse.

You can apply to the Supreme Court for an order dispensing with written consent; however, the court will decide what is in the best interest of the child.

5. Application Process

Applying for a name change is a simple process. You will need to complete the Application for Change of Name and submit it to your local registry. You can find the form at www.hss.gov.nt.ca/sites/default/files/application_for_change_of_name_package.pdf.

Those not born in the Northwest Territories need to contact their former jurisdiction where they were born. That jurisdiction may have different instructions for applying for a new birth certificate with the new name.

5.1 Necessary documents

You will need to provide the registry agent with a proof of identity document (e.g., driver's licence) when you are submitting your name change application. These are the documents you'll need:

- Birth certificate (and any certified copies).
- Court orders for custody (if applying for a child).
- Parental agreements (if applying for a child).
- Separation agreements.
- Written consents (or court order dispensing with written consents).

If you don't provide all the required documents, your application could be delayed or denied.

5.2 Declaration

At the end of the Application for Change of Name you will find a Declaration section. You will need to declare before a Commissioner for Oaths, notary public, or Justice of the Peace for the NWT that what you said in your application is true.

You can find a commissioner, notary, or Justice of the Peace either in the local court house or in the Yellow Pages. There is a fee for this service, which can vary, so shop around to find the most reasonable price.

5.3 Publication of name change

Once your application has been approved, the Registrar General will notify the following:

- Clerk of the Supreme Court.
- RCMP.
- Maintenance Enforcement Administrator.
- NWT Healthcare Registration unit, Health Services Administration.
- Vital Statistics Office of the province of birth (for those not born in the NWT).
- Any other authorities required to receive notification under the government regulations.

The name change will also be published in the *Northwest Territories Gazette* (both paper and online formats).

The Registrar General may decide not to publish the name if the name change is minor (e.g., to correct a typo or error), the person is commonly known under the new name, or the public notice would cause undue hardship (e.g., violent domestic situations) to the person applying for the name change.

6. Cost and Payment Methods

The fees are as follows:

- Change of Name: $125.
- Each additional person included on an adult application: $50.
- Duplicate Change of Name Certificate: $25.
- Statutory Declaration: Use of Common-Law Spouse's Last Name: $20.
- Statutory Declaration: Breakdown of Spousal Relationship: $20.

You can pay by cheque or money order payable to the Government of the Northwest Territories. If you don't have a registry close to you, and you want to pay by credit card, you must submit the application by fax (see section 7. for fax number).

The fee may be waived if the Registrar General considers the name change as necessary in order to avoid hardship to the applicant.

7. Contact

Website:
www.hss.gov.nt.ca/vital-statistics/changing-your-name

Telephone: 867-777-7420
Toll free: 1-800-661-0830
Fax: 867-777-3197 (fax to be used if you're paying by credit card)

Registrar General of Vital Statistics
Department of Health and Social Services
Government of the Northwest Territories
Bag #9 (107 Mackenzie Rd/IDC Building 2nd floor)
Inuvik, NT X0E 0T0

Chapter 8

Nova Scotia

It is a relatively simple process to apply for a formal, legal name change in Nova Scotia. This chapter will provide you with the information you will need.

1. Who Doesn't Require a Legal Name Change?

Not everyone needs to go through the formal process to legally change his or her name in Nova Scotia as you will see in the following sections.

1.1 Marriage

If a person wants to take his or her spouse's name through marriage, the process is simple. Either spouse may choose to use the other's last name, or a combination of the two last names. You can combine the two last names using a hyphen or space. The order of the two names is up to you.

You will need to update all your identification (see Appendix II) by sending the official marriage certificate (or a notarized copy of it) to the various places you'll want your name changed (e.g., credit card companies, Social Insurance). Organizations may have

additional requirements, so you will have to contact them to find out if you'll need to send more than a marriage certificate.

1.2 Divorce

You can formally ask for a legal name change by asking the judge to include a legal name change in your divorce order. You can ask for a name change of any children in your custody at that time as well; however, this is up to the discretion of the judge. You will need the consent of your spouse in order to apply for a name change for your children (see section 4.).

If you're recently divorced, and didn't ask for a name change in your divorce order, you can informally return to the last surname you had before marriage or the name you were given at birth. You will follow the same process as you did when you got married by contacting the various organizations (e.g., banks, credit card companies) and asking what they need in order to change your identification. Many places will need to see the official divorce certificate (or a notarized copy of it) and your birth certificate.

2. Who Is Eligible to Apply?

The following outlines who is eligible to apply for a formal name change:

- A resident of Nova Scotia for at least one year.
- A Canadian citizen.
- A permanent resident.
- A person who has reached the age of majority (19 years old or older).

If you're younger than 19 years of age and you have a child, you can apply as if you were the age of majority. You can also apply to change the name of your own child; however, you may need written consent from the other parent (see section 4.).

If you want to change the name of your spouse, you'll need his or her consent. See Form C — Consent to Change of Name in the download kit included with this book for an example. or visit www.novascotia.ca/just/regulations/regs/changenam.htm. Contact Vital Statistics for your copy (see section 7.).

3. Name Restrictions

There are some restrictions on what type of name you can choose:

- The name must include a first name and surname.
- The surname cannot have more than two components (although surname can be joined by a hyphen).
- Must use the Roman alphabet.
- The name cannot cause confusion, inconvenience, duress, or embarrassment.
- The name cannot be used in a manner to defraud or mislead the public, or to avoid paying your debts.

If you want any type of punctuation (e.g., period, apostrophe, accent), you'll need to contact your local court registry to find out what types are accepted. There may be a limit on the amount of punctuation used in your name as well.

4. Change of Name of a Child

To change the name of a child, he or she must be in your lawful custody. You cannot apply to have a child's name changed if there is a court order, parental agreement, or separation agreement that states the child's name cannot be changed.

If the other parent (or guardian) has lawful custody or access to the child, he or she will need to give his or her written consent in order for you to change the child's name.

You can apply to the court for an order dispensing with written consent if the person whose consent is required cannot be found, he or she is not providing proper care or contributing child support, or the person is of unsound mind or deceased; however, the court will decide what is in the best interest of the child.

If your current spouse is not the biological parent of the child, but you want to change the child's last name to your current spouse's, you'll need the written consent of your spouse.

You may apply to change the name of a child who is mentally incompetent or physically disabled and is 12 years of age or older (including those who have reached the age of majority of 19 years). However, allowing it is up to the discretion of the court.

5. Application Process

Applying for a name change is a simple process. You will need to complete Form B — Application for a Change of Name (see example in the download kit included with this book or visit www. novascotia.ca/just/regulations/regs.changenam.htm. Contact Vital Statistics for your copy (see section **7.**) and submit it to your local registry.

5.1 Necessary documents

You will need to provide the registry agent with a proof of identity document (e.g., driver's licence) when you are submitting your name change application. These are the documents you'll also need:

- Birth certificate and any certified copies (if born outside Nova Scotia).
- Marriage certificate (if married in another province or territory).
- Immigration documents (e.g., Record of Landing).
- Court orders for custody (if applying for a child).
- Parental agreements (if applying for a child).
- Separation agreements.
- Written consents (or court order dispensing with written consents).
- Any other evidence required by the Registrar at the time of application.

For a married person who is not planning on separating or divorcing, but for whatever reason would like to change his or her surname, that person will need the written consent of his or her spouse.

If you don't provide all the required documents, your application could be delayed or denied.

5.2 Statutory declaration

You will need to complete Form D — Statutory Declaration (see example in the download kit included with this book or visit www. novascotia.ca/just/regulations/regs.changenam.htm. Contact Vital

Statistics for your copy (see section 7.). What this means is you will need to declare before a commissioner, notary public, or barrister that what you said in the Application for a Change of Name is true and accurate.

You can find a commissioner, barrister, or notary either at the local court house or in the Yellow Pages. There is a fee for this service, which can vary, so shop around to find the most reasonable price.

5.3 Publication of name change

Once your application has been approved, Vital Statistics may notify the following:

- RCMP, municipal police, and Sheriff.
- Director of Maintenance Enforcement.
- Family court.
- Registry of deeds (in your county).
- Province, territory, or country where you were born.
- Registrar of motor vehicles.
- Any other authorities who are required to receive notification under the government regulations.

The name change will also be published in the *Royal Gazette* (both paper and online formats).

The Director of Vital Statistics may decide not to publish the name if the name change is minor (e.g., a typo or error) or the public notice would cause undue hardship (e.g., violent domestic situations, or where the child is committed permanently to the Director of Child Protection) to the person applying for the name change.

6. Cost and Payment Methods

The fees are as follows:

- Legal change of name: $160.85.
- Each additional change to a birth or marriage record on the same change of name: $24.20.

If you are applying in person, you can pay by cash, debit card, money order, cheque (to the Minister of Finance), American Express, MasterCard, or Visa. If you are applying by mail, the same types of payments are accepted except for cash and debit card.

It takes about two weeks for the application to be processed.

7. Contact

You will need to contact Vital Statistics in Nova Scotia to get a copy of the application and forms you'll need.

Vital Statistics
Service Nova Scotia and Municipal Relations
300 Horseshoe Lake Drive
Halifax, Nova Scotia B3S 0B7

Postal Address:
Service Nova Scotia and Municipal Relations
PO Box 157
Halifax, Nova Scotia B3J 2M9

Telephone: 902-424-4381
Toll free: 1-877-848-2578
Fax: 902-424-0678

Website: www.novascotia.ca/snsmr/access/vitalstats.asp

Chapter 9

Nunavut

It is a relatively simple process to apply for a formal, legal name change in Nunavut. This chapter will provide you with the information you will need.

Note: If you were born before April 1, 1999, you will need to contact the Registrar General of Vital Statistics in the Northwest Territories. See Chapter 7 for more information about applying for a name change in the Northwest Territories.

1. Who Doesn't Require a Legal Name Change?

Not everyone needs to go through the formal process to legally change his or her name in Nunavut as you will see in the following sections.

1.1 Marriage

If a person wants to take his or her spouse's name through marriage, the process is simple. Either spouse may choose to use the other's last name, or a combination of the two last names. You can combine the two last names using a hyphen or space. The order of the two names is up to you.

You will need to update all your identification (see Appendix II) by sending the official marriage certificate (or a notarized copy of it) to the various places you want your name changed (e.g., credit card companies, Social Insurance). Organizations may have additional requirements, so you will have to contact them to find out if you'll need to send more than a marriage certificate.

1.2 Divorce

If you're recently divorced, you can return to the last surname you had before marriage or the name you were given at birth. You will follow the same process as you did when you got married by contacting the various organizations (e.g., banks, credit card companies) and asking what they need in order to change your identification. Many places will need to see the official divorce certificate (or a notarized copy of it) and your birth certificate.

2. Who Is Eligible to Apply?

The following outlines who is eligible to apply for a formal name change:

- A resident in Nunavut (i.e., you have lived in Nunavut for at least one year).
- A Canadian citizen.
- A permanent resident.
- A person who has reached the age of majority (19 years old or older).

If you're younger than 19, you can still apply for a change of name if you:

- Have been a spouse.
- Are currently a spouse.

3. Name Restrictions

There are some restrictions on what type of name you can choose:

- The name must include a first name and surname.
- The surname cannot have more than two components (although surname can be joined by a hyphen).

- The name must use only the Roman alphabet.
- The name cannot include numbers, initials, or symbols.
- The name cannot cause confusion or embarrassment to another person.
- The name cannot be used in a manner to defraud or mislead the public.

If you want any type of punctuation (e.g., a period, an apostrophe, or an accent), you'll need to contact your local court registry to find out what types are accepted. There may be a limit on the amount of punctuation used in your name as well.

4. Change of Name of a Child

To change the name of a child, he or she must be in your lawful custody. You cannot apply to have a child's name changed if there is a court order, parental agreement, or separation agreement that states the child's name cannot be changed.

If the other parent (or guardian) has lawful custody or access to the child, he or she will need to give his or her written consent in order for you to change the child's name. (See the example on the download kit included with this book or visit www.nucj.ca/changename.htm.) It is not necessary to get consent if the other parent doesn't have or share lawful custody, is not contributing child support, or has severed his or her relationship with the child.

You can apply to the court for an order dispensing with written consent if the person whose consent is required cannot be found; however, the court will decide what is in the best interests of the child.

If your current spouse is not the biological parent of the child, but you want to change the child's last name to your current spouse's, you'll need the written consent of your spouse.

If the child is 12 years of age or older, you must have the child's written consent.

You may apply to change the name of a child who is mentally incompetent or physically disabled and is 12 years of age or older (including those who have reached the age of majority of 19 years). However, allowing this is at the discretion of the court.

Complete the change of name form for one child. If you're applying for multiple children, then you will need to complete an additional change of name form (see examples on the download kit included with this book or visit www.nucj.ca/changename.htm).

5. Application Process

Applying for a name change is a simple process. You will need to complete the Change of Name application (see examples on the download kit included with this book or visit www.nucj.ca/changename.htm) and submit it to your local registry.

Those who were not born in Nunavut need to contact their former jurisdiction where they were born. That jurisdiction may have different instructions for applying for a new birth certificate with the new name. Note that if you were born before April 1, 1999, you will need to contact the NWT Registrar General of Vital Statistics (see section 7. for contact information).

5.1 Necessary documents

You will need to provide the registry agent with two proof of identity documents (e.g., driver's licence and a birth certificate) when you are submitting your name change application. If you don't have two pieces of ID, you may ask someone who has known you for a long time to swear an affidavit confirming that you are who you say you are. These are the documents you'll need to include with your application:

- Birth certificate (and any certified copies).
- Baptismal certificate (if applicable).
- Court orders for custody (if applying for a child).
- Parental agreements (if applying for a child).
- Separation agreements.
- Written consents (or court order dispensing with written consents).
- A certificate of a Sheriff if there are any unsatisfied property disputes (e.g., liens, pending actions), where a name change could cause problems for the other property owners.

If you don't provide all the required documents, your application could be delayed or denied.

5.2 Affidavit

Your Change of Name application is also an affidavit. What this means is you will need to swear or affirm before a Commissioner for Oaths or notary public in and for Nunavut Territory that what you said in the application is true.

You can find a commissioner or notary either in the local court house or in the Yellow Pages. There is a fee for this service, which can vary, so shop around to find the most reasonable price.

5.3 Publication of name change

Once your application has been approved, the clerk of the court will notify the following:

- Registrar General of Vital Statistics.
- Sheriff (in the appropriate jurisdiction).
- Any other authorities who are required to receive notification under the government regulations.

The name change will also be published in the *Nunavut Gazette* (both paper and online formats).

It may be decided not to publish the name if the name change is minor (e.g., correction of a typo or error) or the public notice would cause undue hardship (e.g., violent domestic situations) to the person applying for the name change. Please check with the court clerk if you think you have cause for not having your change of name information published.

6. Cost and Payment Methods

The application fee is $10, which must be paid when you are submitting the application. Ask the court clerk what type of payment methods are currently accepted.

7. Contact

Nunavut Vital Statistics
Bag 3
Rankin Inlet, Nunavut X0C 0G0

Telephone: 867-645-8002
Fax: 867-645-8092
Toll free: 1-800-661-0833

Email: info@gov.nu.ca

If you were born before April 1, 1999, see Chapter 7 because you will need to apply to the Registrar General of Vital Statistics in the Northwest Territories:

Registrar General of Vital Statistics
Department of Health and Social Services
Government of the Northwest Territories
Bag #9 (107 Mackenzie Rd/IDC Building 2nd floor)
Inuvik, NT X0E 0T0

Website:
www.hss.gov.nt.ca/vital-statistics/changing-your-name

Telephone: 867-777-7420
Toll free: 1-800-661-0830
Fax: 867-777-3197 (fax to be used if you're paying by credit card)

Chapter 10

Ontario

It is a relatively simple process to apply for a formal, legal name change in Ontario. This chapter will provide you with the information you will need.

1. Who Doesn't Require a Legal Name Change?

Not everyone needs to go through the formal process to legally change his or her name in Ontario as you will see in the following sections.

1.1 Marriage

If a person wants to take his or her spouse's name through marriage, the *informal* process is simple. Either spouse may choose to use the other's last name, or a combination of the two last names. You can combine the two last names by using a hyphen. The order of the two names is up to you.

You will need to update all your identification (see Appendix II) by sending the official marriage certificate (or a notarized copy of it) to the various places you want your name changed (e.g., credit card companies, Social Insurance). Organizations may have additional requirements, so you will have to contact them to find out if you'll need to send more than a marriage certificate.

If you want to *formally* change your last name (i.e., change your birth records), you can do so for free within 90 days of marriage. After 90 days a formal change to your married name will cost $25.

1.2 Divorce

If you're recently divorced, you can return to the last surname you had before marriage or the surname you were given at birth. You will do the same process as you did when you were married by contacting the various organizations (e.g., banks, credit card companies) and asking what they need in order to change your identification. Many places will need to see the official divorce certificate (or a notarized copy of it) and your birth certificate.

1.3 Name change election

You will need to contact the Office of the Registrar General for the Name Change Election form if you want to *formally* change your surname in the following circumstances:

- Marriage.
- Divorce.
- Death of your spouse.
- Living in a common-law relationship (same sex or opposite sex).

For common-law couples, you'll need to also submit a Joint Declaration of Conjugal Relationship; will need to contact Service Ontario for this.

2. Who Is Eligible to Apply?

The following outlines who is eligible to apply for a formal name change:

- A resident of Ontario (i.e., you must have lived in Ontario for at least 12 months).
- A Canadian citizen.
- A permanent resident.

- A person who has reached the age of majority (18 years old or older).

If you're 16 or 17 years of age and you're married, or you're no longer under the legal custody of someone else, you can apply to change your name without your parents' permission.

3. Name Restrictions

There are some restrictions on what type of name you can choose:

- The name must include a first name and surname.
- The surname cannot have more than two components (surname can be joined by a hyphen).
- The name must use only the Roman alphabet.
- The name cannot include numbers, initials, or symbols.
- The name cannot cause confusion or embarrassment to another person.
- The name cannot be used in a manner to defraud or mislead the public.

If you want any type of punctuation (e.g., a period, an apostrophe, or an accent), you'll need to contact ServiceOntario to find out what types are accepted. There may be a limit to the amount of punctuation used in your name as well.

4. Change of Name of a Child

To change the name of a child, he or she must be in your lawful custody. You cannot apply to have a child's name changed if there is a court order, parental agreement, or separation agreement that denies the child's name to be changed.

If the other parent (or guardian) has lawful custody or access to the child, he or she will need to give his or her written consent in order for you to change the child's name.

You can apply to the court for an order dispensing with written consent if the person whose consent is required cannot be found, is not providing proper care or contributing child support, or is of unsound mind or deceased; however, the court will decide what is in the best interest of the child.

If the child is 12 years of age or older, you must have the child's written consent.

If your current spouse is not the biological parent of the child, but you want to change the child's last name to your current spouse's, you'll need the written consent of your spouse.

You may apply to change the name of a child who is mentally incompetent or physically disabled who is 12 years of age or older (including a child who has reached the age of majority of 18 or older). However, allowing the change is up to the discretion of the court. You will need to ask a qualified medical practitioner to state in writing — not more than one year before the name change application is made — that in his or her professional opinion the child does not have the capacity to consent.

The Application to Change a Child's Name form can be found online (www.forms.ssb.gov.on.ca/mbs/ssb/forms/ssbforms. nsf/AttachDownload?openagent&TM=1_28_2014_6_25_43_ PM&ENV=WWE&NO=007-11156E&SEQ=3&VER=1).

5. Application Process

Applying for a name change is a simple process. You will need to complete the Application to Change an Adult's Name and submit it to ServiceOntario. You can find the form online (www.forms. ssb.gov.on.ca/mbs/ssb/forms/ssbforms.nsf/AttachDownload?op enagent&TM=1_28_2014_6_22_31PM&ENV=WWE&NO=007-11155E&SEQ=3&VER=3). There is an example included in the download that came with this book.

5.1 Necessary documents

Along with your completed application you will need to include the following documents (if applicable to your situation):

- Birth certificate and any certified copies.
- Marriage certificate.
- Divorce certificate.
- Immigration documents (e.g., Canadian citizenship certificate, Landed Immigrant or Permanent Resident certificates).
- Court orders for custody (if applying for a child).

- Parental agreements (if applying for a child).
- Separation agreements.
- Written consents (or court order dispensing with written consents).
- Court certified copies of court orders.
- Financial statements if you are listed as a borrower or debtor.
- Bankruptcy documents (if you're an undischarged bankrupt).
- Documentation about liens against or security interests to do with your personal property.
- Photocopies of previous name change certificates.
- Any other evidence required by the Registrar at the time of application.

In some circumstances ServiceOntario may request to see original or certified copies instead of photocopies.

If you have any outstanding court proceedings or criminal charges, you will need to contact your local police department to obtain a police records check and submit it with your application. The types of situations that will need a police records check include the following:

- If you have ever committed a criminal offence and been convicted. (If you had a pardon granted, a police records check is not necessary.)
- If you've ever had a warrant issued for you.
- If you have ever had a restraining order against you.
- If you have ever had your driver's licence suspended.
- If you are under a parole order.
- If you have any pending charges against you.

5.2 Guarantor's statement

To prove that you've lived in Ontario for 12 months or longer, you will need a guarantor to sign pages 11 and 12 of the change of name application. A guarantor must be a resident of Ontario and he or she cannot be a relative. A professional guarantor includes:

- Provincial judge.
- Justice of the peace.
- Chief of Indian bands.
- Persons authorized to solemnize marriages.
- Medical practitioner.
- Members of the Law Society.
- Head of a municipal council.
- Municipal clerks.
- Principal of an elementary or a secondary school.
- Bank manager or bank signing officer.

If you don't know anyone who is considered a professional guarantor, you can ask someone who has known you for a minimum of five years.

5.3 Statutory declaration

On page 16 of the application you will find a Statutory Declaration form. This means you are declaring before a Commissioner for Taking Affidavits or a Commissioner for Taking Oaths that what you said in your application is true and accurate.

You can find a commissioner at the local court house. You can also contact ServiceOntario for a list of commissioners. There is a fee for this service, which can vary, so shop around to find the most reasonable price.

5.4 Publication of name change

Once your application has been approved, Vital Statistics may notify the following:

- RCMP, municipal police, and Sheriff.
- Director of Maintenance Enforcement.
- Registrar of the court (e.g., family court, criminal court).
- Province, territory, or country where you were born.
- Registrar of motor vehicles.

- Registrar of Personal Property Security.
- Registrar in Bankruptcy.
- Any other authorities who are required to receive notification under the government regulations.

The name change will also be published in *The Ontario Gazette* (both paper and online formats). ServiceOntario may decide not to publish the name if the person is a transgendered individual and requests that publication not be made; or the public notice would cause undue hardship (e.g., violent domestic situations) to the person applying for the name change. Contact ServiceOntario if either of these situations apply to you and ask for the form titled Request for Non-Publication in *The Ontario Gazette*.

6. Cost and Payment Methods

The fees are as follows:

- Application to Change a Child's Name: $137.
- Application to Change an Adult's Name: $137.
- To amend a child's name (younger than 12) to something he or she could have been given at the time of birth (i.e., the father's last name): $37.
- To change a child's name at the same time as the parent changes his or her name (applications must be submitted together): $22 per child.

The payment methods include cheque (payable to the Minister of Finance), money order, Visa, MasterCard, or American Express.

7. Contact

Your application can take six to eight weeks to process. If there are errors, the process will take longer.

You can contact ServiceOntario in the following ways:

Office of the Registrar General, ServiceOntario
PO Box 3000
189 Red River Road
Thunder Bay, ON P7B 5W0

Telephone: 416-325-8305
Toll free: 1-800-461-2156
Fax: 807-343-7459

Website: www.ontario.ca/welcome-serviceontario

Chapter 11

Prince Edward Island

It is a relatively simple process to apply for a formal, legal name change in Prince Edward Island. This chapter will provide you with the information you will need.

1. Who Doesn't Require a Legal Name Change?

Not everyone needs to go through the formal process to legally change his or her name in Prince Edward Island as you will see in the following sections.

1.1 Marriage

If a person wants to take his or her spouse's name through marriage, the process is simple. Either spouse may choose to use the other's last name, or a combination of the two last names. You can combine the two last names using a hyphen or space. The order of the two names is up to you.

You will need to update all your identification (see Appendix II) by sending the official marriage certificate (or a notarized copy of it) to the various places you want your name changed (e.g., credit card companies, Social Insurance). Organizations may have

additional requirements, so you will have to contact them to find out if you'll need to send more than a marriage certificate.

1.2 Divorce

If you're recently divorced, you can return to the last surname you had before marriage or the name you were given at birth. You will follow the same process as you did when you got married by contacting the various organizations (e.g., banks, credit card companies) and asking what they need in order to change your identification. Many places will need to see the official divorce certificate (or a notarized copy of it) and your birth certificate.

2. Who Is Eligible to Apply?

The following outlines who is eligible to apply for a formal name change:

- A resident of PE (i.e., you have lived in PE for three consecutive months preceding the change of name application).
- A Canadian citizen.
- A permanent resident.
- A person who has reached the age of majority (18 years or older).
- A person who is not in the lawful custody of another person (e.g., emancipated minor).

3. Name Restrictions

There are some restrictions on what type of name you can choose:

- The name must include a first name and surname.
- The surname cannot have more than two components (although surname can be joined by a hyphen).
- The name must use only the Roman alphabet.
- The name cannot include numbers, initials, or symbols.
- The name cannot cause confusion or embarrassment to another person.
- The name cannot be used in a manner to defraud or mislead the public.

If you want any type of punctuation (e.g., period, apostrophe, accent), you'll need to contact your local registry or Vital Statistics to find out what types are accepted. There may be a limit to the amount of punctuation that you may use in your name.

4. Change of Name of a Child

To change the name of a child, he or she must be in your lawful custody. You cannot apply to have a child's name changed if there is a court order, parental agreement, or separation agreement that states the child's name cannot be changed.

If the other parent (or guardian) has lawful custody or access to the child, he or she will need to give his or her written consent in order for you to change the child's name.

You can apply to the court for an order dispensing with written consent if the person whose consent is required cannot be found, has severed his or her relationship with the child, or refuses to give consent. The court will decide what is in the best interest of the child.

If the child is 12 years of age or older, you must have the child's written consent.

5. Application Process

You cannot apply online for a legal name change in PE. You have to contact Vital Statistics to acquire the forms needed for the application process. When you are done completing the forms, you will follow Vital Statistics' process for submitting the forms. See section **7.** for Vital Statistics' contact information.

You will need to know the following information in order to complete the name change application process:

- The complete names, both present and proposed.
- Place and date of birth.
- Any previous change of name details.
- Address and length of ordinary residence in the province (must be at least three months).

5.1 Necessary documents

You will need to provide Vital Statistics with a proof of identity document (e.g., driver's licence) when you are submitting your name change application. These are the documents you may also need to include:

- Birth certificate (and any certified copies).
- Court orders for custody (if applying for a child).
- Parental agreements (if applying for a child).
- Separation agreements.
- Marriage certificate.
- Written consents (or court order dispensing with written consents).
- Baptismal certificate (if applicable).

If you don't provide all the required documents, your application could be delayed or denied.

5.2 Publication of name change

Once your application has been approved, Vital Statistics will notify the following:

- RCMP, municipal police, and Sheriff.
- Director of Maintenance Enforcement.
- Family court.
- Registry of deeds (in your county).
- Province, territory, or country where you were born.
- Registrar of motor vehicles.
- Any other authorities who are required to receive notification under the government regulations.

The name change will also be published in the *Royal Gazette* (both paper and online formats).

The Director of Vital Statistics may decide not to publish the name if the name change is minor (e.g., correction of a typo or error) or the public notice would cause undue hardship to the person applying for the name change (e.g., violent domestic situations, or if the child committed permanently to the Director of Child Protection).

6. Cost and Payment Methods

The fees are as follows:

- Administering a change of name (18 years of age or older): $192.40
- Administering a change of name (minor): $115.90
- Change of name certificate (per each extra copy): $35.00
- Registering a change of name that has taken place outside PE: $25.00

For methods of payment, please contact Vital Statistics.

7. Contact

You will need to contact Vital Statistics for a change of name application package.

Vital Statistics
126 Douses Road
Montague, PE C0A 1R0

Telephone: 902-838-0880
Toll free: 1-877-320-1253
Fax: 902-838-0883

Website: www.gov.pe.ca/vitalstatistics

Chapter 12

Québec

In Québec, the rules for who can apply and who may actually be allowed to legally change his or her name can vary significantly from those in other Canadian provinces and territories. This chapter will provide you with the information you will need.

1. Marriage and Divorce in Québec

If a person wants to take his or her spouse's name through marriage, the process is simple in the rest of Canada. Either spouse may choose to use the other's last name, or a combination of the two last names. You can even combine the two last names using a hyphen or space. The order of the two names is up to you.

However, in Québec, a 1981 provincial law forbids a spouse taking the other spouse's last name, even through official, legal name change channels (article 393 of the Civil Code of Québec; this can be seen at www2.publicationsduquebec.gouv.qc.ca/dynamic-Search/telecharge.php?type=2&file=/CCQ_1991/CCQ1991_A.html).

Obviously, this means that if you're getting divorced, you won't need to return to your previous name since if you got married in

Québec, you won't have assumed your spouse's name. If you were married elsewhere you should follow the steps for a legal, formal change of name.

2. Who Is Eligible to Apply?

The following outlines who is eligible to apply for a formal name change:

- A resident of Québec for at least the previous one year.
- Someone who is 18 years of age or older.
- You can apply for a name change if it is your own name.
- You can apply to change your child's name (you'll need a birth certificate showing parentage; the child must be younger than 18 and it can only be filed by the child's mother, father, or tutor if applicable; if the child is older than 14 he or she must consent).

If you were born outside of Québec, and your birth was not entered in the Québec register of civil status, you must first ask the Directeur de l'état civil to insert the act of birth in the register so the application for your change of name can be processed. Complete the Application for Insertion of an Act of Civil Status Made Outside Québec in the Québec Register of Civil Status form (see Sample 27 for a sample of the amendment form). Follow the instructions on the form carefully. You can obtain it from www. etatcivil.gouv.qc.ca/en/change-name.html#significant. See also the download kit included with this book.

If you are a temporary resident (e.g., work or student visa), or tourist/visitor, you cannot apply for a name change in Québec.

Again, it is important to note that Québec does not allow for spouses to take each other's names upon marriage, so applying for a legal name change to a spouse's name likely will not be allowed. What would likely be allowed is a correction to spelling, or a name change was desired because perhaps you have the same name as someone famous and that person has been doing things with which you do not want to be associated. Whether or not a name change will be allowed is up to the discretion of the Directeur.

3. Name Restrictions

There are some restrictions on what type of name you can choose:

- You must include a first and last name.
- The name has to use the Roman alphabet.
- The name cannot have non-letter characters (i.e., no symbols).
- The name cannot include profanity.
- The name cannot include numbers.

If you want to have an accent in your name, you will need to contact the registry to find out what accents are acceptable, if they are not accents normally found in the French language. There may also be a limit to the amount of punctuation marks and accents that will be accepted; contact the registry if you wish to use punctuation marks to find out what are acceptable such as a period, a hyphen, and an apostrophe.

4. Application Process

The first step is to complete the Request for Preliminary Analysis for a Change of Name Application form. This can be found here: www.etatcivil.gouv.qc.ca/publications/FO-12-04-request-preliminary-analysis-modification-surname-first-name.pdf. See also the download kit included with this book for an example.

Once you have completed and submitted this form, the office will let you know whether you are eligible to continue with the process of applying to legally change your name. If you are, they will send you a package of the forms with which to do so. If not, they will let you know your options.

Note that even if you are found eligible to apply, it does not mean that the Directeur de l'état civil will approve the name change; all decisions are up to the Directeur in Québec.

It can take up to 90 days to process your application, and once it is all final, you will need to update all your identification (see Appendix II) by sending your Change of Name certificate (or a copy of it; check individual requirements) to the various places you want your name changed (e.g., credit card companies, Social Insurance).

Organizations may have additional requirements, so you will have to contact them to find out what you need to show them.

4.1 Necessary documents

You will need to show your original Canadian birth certificate. If you don't have the original, you can get a notarized copy of your Canadian birth certificate. If you were born in Québec, and you don't have an original birth certificate, Vital Statistics will find the original on file for you. You're required to include with the application all original birth certificates.

People who were not born in Québec will have to contact their former jurisdiction where they were born. That jurisdiction may have different instructions for applying for a new birth certificate with the new name.

Each situation is different, but you also may be required to provide the following when applying to legally change your name in Québec, so be prepared and follow the instructions on the forms:

- Marriage certificates (original certificates and not the civil or religious marriage certificates).
- Written consents (if you are changing the name of a child, partner, or spouse).
- Dispensations.
- Affidavit.
- Proof of marital status.
- Court order.
- Guardianship order.
- Affidavit of Sole Guardianship.
- Notarized translation of documents (including an affidavit affirmed or sworn by a translator).

For those born outside of Canada, you will need a Canadian citizenship certificate or Permanent Resident Card.

If you have previously had a legal name change, you must disclose this information. You will also need a copy of all your previous Change of Name Certificates.

4.2 Publication of name change

According to Québec law, all registered name changes must be published in the *Gazette officielle du Québec* and in a local newspaper (this law may be changing soon; check with the Directeur de l'état civil for current requirements).

At the time of writing, anyone who submits an application for a change of name to the Directeur de l'état civil must give public notice of their intention to change their name by publishing it at least four times:

- Two notices must be published, seven days apart, in the *Gazette officielle du Québec* (the notices are also published on its website).

- Two notices must be published, seven days apart, in a local newspaper published in the judicial district where the person concerned by the application is domiciled.

- If the application for a change of name concerns the applicant and the applicant's child, two more notices must be published, seven days apart, in the local newspaper published in the judicial district where the child is domiciled, if different from the district where the applicant is domiciled.

If there is a reason you don't want your new name published (e.g., due to someone stalking you or violent domestic situations), the justice minister may grant a special exemption; contact the Directeur de l'état civil for more information.

5. Cost

The government fees at time of writing are:

- Surname or given name change for one person only (adult or child, including issuance of the first Change of Name Certificate): $133.00.

- Surname change for a child younger than 18, when included with surname change for the parent (including issuance of the first Change of Name Certificate): $26.75.

- Issuance of a Change of Name Certificate: $10.70.

If swearing or affirming of any affidavits are necessary, a commissioner or notary will have a fee, which can vary, so shop around.

6. Contact

If you have questions, you can talk to the Directeur de l'état civil:

Website: www.etatcivil.gouv.qc.ca/en/default.html, or
www.etatcivil.gouv.qc.ca/en/change-name.html

Email: etatcivil@dec.gouv.qc.ca

Telephone: 418-644-4545 or 514-644-4545
Toll free: 1-877-644-4545

Mail:
Le Directeur de l'état civil
2535, boulevard Laurier
Québec, QC G1V 5C5

Chapter 13

Saskatchewan

It is a relatively simple process to apply for a formal, legal name change in Saskatchewan. This chapter will provide you with the information you will need.

1. Who Doesn't Require a Legal Name Change?

Not everyone needs to go through the formal process to legally change his or her name in Saskatchewan as you will see in the following sections.

1.1 Marriage

If a person wants to take his or her spouse's name through marriage, the process is simple. Either spouse may choose to use the other's last name, or a combination of the two last names. You can combine the two last names using a hyphen or space. The order of the two names is up to you.

You will need to update all your identification (see Appendix II) by sending the official marriage certificate (or a notarized copy of it) to the various places you want your name changed (e.g., credit card companies, Social Insurance). Organizations may have

additional requirements, so you will have to contact them to find out if you'll need to send more than a marriage certificate.

1.2 Divorce, annulment, or widowed

If you're recently divorced or widowed, or a marriage has been annulled, you can return to the last name you had before marriage. You will follow the same process as you did when you got married by contacting the various organizations (e.g., banks, credit card companies) and asking what they need in order to change your identification. Many places will need to see the official divorce certificate (or a notarized copy of it) and your birth certificate.

1.3 Amendment of a name

In some circumstances, a person can correct his or her name without completing the legal name change process. At the time of birth, registration is completed and filed permanently with Vital Statistics. If the registration includes incomplete, missing, or incorrect information, you can request to correct it.

If you were not born in Saskatchewan, you will need to contact Vital Statistics or a similar agency in the jurisdiction where you were born.

2. Who Is Eligible to Apply?

The following outlines who is eligible to apply for a formal name change:

- A resident of Saskatchewan.
- Someone who is 18 years of age or older.
- You can apply for a name change if it is your own name.
- You can change your spouse's name (you'll need a marriage certificate and his or her consent).
- Child's name (you'll need a birth certificate showing parentage; custody; and the child must be younger than 18 and give his or her consent if 14 or older).

If you're younger than the age of 18, you may still change your name if one or more of the following applies:

- You're legally married.
- You're living in an adult interdependent relationship.
- You're the parent of a child.
- You're the guardian of a child.

If you are a temporary resident (e.g., work or student visa), or tourist/visitor, you cannot apply for a name change in Saskatchewan.

3. Name Restrictions

There are some restrictions on what type of name you can choose:

- You must include a first and last name.
- The name has to use the Roman alphabet.
- The name cannot have non-letter characters (i.e., no symbols).
- The name cannot include profanity.
- The name cannot include numbers.

Some punctuation marks are acceptable, such as a period, a hyphen, and an apostrophe. If you want to have an accent in your name, you will need to contact the registry to find out what accents are acceptable. There is also a limit to the amount of punctuation marks and accents that will be accepted.

4. Application Process

You cannot apply online for a legal name change in Saskatchewan. You can call eHealth's Customer Support Team toll-free at 1-855-eHS-LINK (347-5465) or go in person to the Regina Customer Service Centre at 2130 11th Avenue, Regina, Saskatchewan S4P 0J5 to obtain the application.

4.1 Necessary documents

You will need to bring your original Canadian birth certificate. If you don't have the original, you can use a notarized copy of your Canadian birth certificate. If you were born in Saskatchewan, and you don't have an original birth certificate, Vital Statistics will find the original on file for you. You're required to include with the application all original birth certificates.

People who were not born in Saskatchewan will need to contact their former jurisdiction where they were born. That jurisdiction may have different instructions for applying for a new birth certificate with the new name.

You will need to provide the registry agent with these documents:

- Proof of residency for yourself and everyone whose name appears on the application — copies of Saskatchewan Health Cards usually suffice.

- An official birth certificate for each person whose name is to be changed as long as those birth certificates were issued in Canada or the United States — if a person was born elsewhere, official Certificates of Canadian Citizenship or official immigration documents must be submitted.

- A completed Change of Name Application form and the written consent of those whose names will be affected by the application (if required).

- An official marriage certificate (if you are married).

- An official death certificate (if you are widowed).

- An official or a certified photocopy of a Certificate of Divorce (if you are divorced).

- An official or a certified photocopy of any agreement, judgment, Decree Nisi or other court order granted with respect to the custody of any child(ren) named in the application.

- An affidavit signed before a Notary Public, Justice of the Peace, or Commissioner for Oaths declaring that the statements made in the application for change of name are true.

Those born outside of Canada will need a Canadian citizenship certificate or Permanent Resident Card. The registry will not accept the following documents from those born outside Canada:

- Social Insurance card.

- Notice of birth registration.

- Baptismal certificate.

- Immigration documents.

- Passport.

- Driver's licence.

- Commemoration of Canadian citizenship.

- Health-care card.

If you have previously had a legal name change, you must disclose this information. You will also need a copy of all your previous Change of Name Certificates. However, if you have completed the previous change of name in Saskatchewan, Vital Statistics will have access to this in its records.

4.2 Publication of name change

According to the *Vital Statistics Act*, all registered name changes will be published in the *Saskatchewan Gazette* unless it is for a child younger than 15 or there are other special circumstances. The *Gazette* can be seen at www.qp.gov.sk.ca.

4.3 Affidavit

As part of the change of name application, you will find an Affidavit of Qualification and Bona Fides, in which you will need to swear or affirm that what you said in your application is true. You will need to take it to a Commissioner for Oaths or a notary public in Saskatchewan to have it properly sworn or affirmed.

You can find a commissioner or notary either in the local court house or in the Yellow Pages for an independent notary service. There is a fee for this service, which can vary, so shop around to find the most reasonable price.

5. Cost and Payment Methods

The government fees at the time of writing are as follows:

- $125.00: Application Fee (which includes one Change of Name Certificate showing all registered name changes).

- $10.70: Advertising Fee* (for the first name listed on application).

- $3.21: Advertising Fee* (for each subsequent name listed on application).

- * No advertising fee is charged for children younger than 15 years of age.

Payments should be made at the time the application is submitted and may be by cheque payable to eHealth Saskatchewan, money order, or credit card (Visa or MasterCard).

The swearing or affirming of the affidavit by a commissioner or notary will have a fee, which can vary so shop around.

6. Contact

A Change of Name Application form may be obtained by contacting the eHealth Customer Support Team.

Website:
www.ehealthsask.ca/vitalstats/Pages/default.aspx

Toll free: 855-347-5465
Fax: 306-787-2288

Email: VitalStatistics@ehealthsask.ca

Mail:
eHealth Saskatchewan
Vital Statistics Registry
2130 11th Avenue
Regina, SK S4P 0J5

Chapter 14

Yukon

It is a relatively simple process to apply for a formal, legal name change in Yukon. This chapter will provide you with the information you will need.

1. Who Doesn't Require a Legal Name Change?

Not everyone needs to go through the formal process to legally change his or her name in Yukon as you will see in the following sections.

1.1 Marriage

If a person wants to take his or her spouse's name through marriage, the process is simple. Either spouse may choose to use the other's last name, or a combination of the two last names. You can combine the two last names using a hyphen or space. The order of the two names is up to you.

You will need to update all your identification (see Appendix II) by sending the official marriage certificate (or a notarized copy of it) to the various places you want your name changed (e.g., credit card companies, Social Insurance). Organizations may have

additional requirements, so you will have to contact them to find out if you'll need to send more than a marriage certificate.

1.2 Divorce

If you're recently divorced, you can return to the last name you had before marriage. You will follow the same process as you did when you got married by contacting the various organizations (e.g., banks, credit card companies) and asking what they need in order to change your identification. Many places will need to see the official divorce certificate (or a notarized copy of it) and your birth certificate.

1.3 Amendment of a name

In some circumstances, a person can correct his or her name without completing the legal name change process. At the time of birth, registration is completed and filed permanently with Vital Statistics. If the registration includes incomplete, missing, or incorrect information, you can request to correct it.

If you were not born in Yukon, you will need to contact Vital Statistics or a similar agency in the jurisdiction where you were born.

You can contact a registry agent in your area or contact Vital Statistics directly for an amendment; complete the Statutory Declaration Re: Error or Omission in Registration form available from Vital Statistics.

2. Who Is Eligible to Apply?

The following outlines who is eligible to apply for a formal name change:

- A resident of Yukon, for at least the preceding three-month period.

- Someone who is 19 years of age or older; or married, widowed, or divorced; or someone who is 18 ½ and living on his or her own (i.e., no longer with a parent or guardian).

- You can apply for a name change if it is your own name.

- You can apply to change a child's name (you'll need a birth certificate showing parentage or custody; the child must be younger than 19 and give his or her consent if 12 or older; children's surnames can only be changed to the surname of his or her mother, father, or other person having custody, or a hyphenated version of any two of those surnames).

If you are a temporary resident (e.g., work or student visa), or tourist/visitor, you cannot apply for a name change in Yukon.

3. Name Restrictions

There are some restrictions on what type of name you can choose:

- You must include a first and last name.
- The name has to use the Roman alphabet.
- The name cannot have non-letter characters (i.e., no symbols).
- The name cannot include profanity.
- The name cannot include numbers.

Some punctuation marks are acceptable such as a period, a hyphen, and an apostrophe. If you want to have an accent in your name, you will need to contact the registry to find out what accents are acceptable. There is also a limit to the amount of punctuation marks and accents that will be accepted.

4. Application Process

You cannot apply online for a legal name change in Yukon. You have to contact a registry and ask for the forms, at which point the registry agent will confirm that you will receive the correct forms; Yukon has forms for name changes for adults, children, or for changing your maiden name to a married one or married to maiden. When you are done completing the forms, you have to return the forms to a registry agent. See the example forms on the download kit included with this book, but please contact Vital Statistics for your application (see section **6.**).

4.1 Necessary documents

You will need to show your original Canadian birth certificate. If you don't have the original, you can get a notarized copy of your Canadian birth certificate. If you were born in Yukon, and you don't have an original birth certificate, Vital Statistics will find the original on file for you. You're required to include with the application all original birth certificates.

People who were not born in Yukon will have to contact their former jurisdiction where they were born. That jurisdiction may have different instructions for applying for a new birth certificate with the new name.

You will need to provide the registry agent with a proof of identity document when you are submitting your name change application. These are the requirements:

- Issued by a government body (e.g., driver's licence, Permanent Residency Card, Canadian citizenship certificate, Status card).
- Must include the person's full name.
- Must include the person's photo.
- Contains a distinct identification number.

Each situation is different, but you also may be required to provide the following:

- Marriage certificates (original certificates and not the civil or religious marriage certificates).
- Written consents (part of the application form if you are changing the name of a child, partner, or spouse).
- Proof of marital status.
- Court order.
- Guardianship order.

For those born outside of Canada, you will need a Canadian citizenship certificate or Permanent Resident Card. The registry will not accept the following documents from those born outside Canada:

- Social Insurance card.
- Notice of birth registration.
- Baptismal certificate.
- Immigration documents.
- Passport.

- Driver's licence.
- Commemoration of Canadian citizenship.
- Health-care card.

If you have previously had a legal name change, you must disclose this information. You will also need a copy of all your previous Change of Name Certificates.

4.2 Publication of name change

According to the law, all registered name changes must be published in the *Yukon Gazette* in both the online and paper formats.

If there is a reason you don't want your new name published (e.g., due to someone stalking you or violent domestic situations), you may be able to request dispensing with publication. Ask a Vital Statistics agent for assistance.

4.3 Affidavit

As part of your change of name application, you will need to fill out an Affidavit of Qualification and Bona Fides (supplied by the registry), in which you will need to swear or affirm that what you said in your application is true. You will need to take it to a Commissioner for Oaths or a notary public in Yukon to have it properly sworn or affirmed.

You can find a commissioner or notary either in the local court house, or look in the Yellow Pages for an independent notary service. There is a fee for this service, which can vary, so shop around to find the most reasonable price.

5. Cost and Payment Methods

The government fee is $50 for a legal change of name, for a new birth certificate, payable by cheque, money order, credit card (Visa, Mastercard, American Express), Interac, or cash (do not mail cash). To change names of additional family members after the initial name change, it costs $17.50 per person.

The swearing or affirming of the affidavit by a commissioner or notary will have a fee, which can vary, so shop around.

6. Contact

If you have questions, you can talk to your local registry, or you can contact Vital Statistics:

Website: www.hss.gov.yk.ca/vitalstats.php

Telephone: 867-667-5207
Toll free: 1-800-661-0408 (extension: 5207)
Fax: 867-393-6486

Email: Vital.Statistics@gov.yk.ca

Mail:
Vital Statistics
Box 2703
Whitehorse, YK Y1A 2C6

Couriers and Walk-ins: 4th floor–204 Lambert Street
Whitehorse, YK Y1A 3T2

Appendix I

Resources

Please note that addresses, phone numbers, email addresses, and web links were current at the time of publication but are subject to change.

Vital Statistics Offices

Alberta

Service Alberta
Vital Statistics
Box 2023
Edmonton, AB T5J 4W7

Telephone: 780-427-7013 (Edmonton and surrounding areas)
Toll free: 310-0000 then dial 780-427-7013

Website: www.servicealberta.gov.ab.ca/1641.cfm

British Columbia

British Columbia Vital Statistics Agency
PO Box 9657 STN PROV GOVT
Victoria, BC V8W 9P3

Telephone: 604-660-2937 or 250-952-2681
Toll free: 1-888-876-1633

Website: www.vs.gov.bc.ca
www.vs.gov.bc.ca/name/

Manitoba

Vital Statistics Agency
254 Portage Avenue
Winnipeg, MB R3C 0B6

Telephone: 204-945-3701
Telephone toll free within Canada: 1-866-949-9296
Fax: 204-948-3128

Website: vitalstats.gov.mb.ca

New Brunswick

Vital Statistics
Service New Brunswick
PO Box 1998
Fredericton, NB E3B 5G4

Telephone: 506-453-2385
Toll free: 1-888-762-8600
Fax: 506-444-4139

Website: www.snb.ca/e/1000/1000-01/e/index-e.asp

Newfoundland and Labrador

Service NL
Vital Statistics Division
Department of Government of Services
PO Box 8700
St. John's, NL A1B 4J6

Telephone: 709-729-3308
Fax: 709-729-0946

Website: www.servicenl.gov.nl.ca/department/ branches/
divisions/vs.html

Northwest Territories

Registrar General of Vital Statistics
Department of Health and Social Services
Government of NWT
Bag#9 (107 Mackenzie Road/IDC Building 2nd floor)
Inuvik, NT X0E 0T0

Telephone: 867-777-7420
Toll free: 1-800-661-0830
Fax: 867-777-3197
(only use the fax if you're paying by credit card)

Website:
www.hss.gov.nt.ca/vital-statistics/changing-your-name

Nova Scotia

Vital Statistics
Service Nova Scotia and Municipal Relations
300 Horseshoe Lake Drive
Halifax, NS B3S 0B7

Postal Address:
Service Nova Scotia and Municipal Relations
PO Box 157
Halifax, NS B3J 2M9

Telephone: 902-424-4381
Toll free: 1-877-848-2578
Fax: 902-424-0678

Website: www.novascotia.ca/snsmr/access/vitalstats.asp

Nunavut

Nunavut Vital Statistics
Bag 3
Rankin Inlet, NU X0C 0G0

Telephone: 867-645-8002
Toll free: 1-800-661-0833
Fax: 867-645-8092

Email: info@gov.nu.ca

Ontario

Office of the Registrar General, ServiceOntario
PO Box 3000
189 Red River Road
Thunder Bay, ON P7B 5W0

Telephone: 416-325-8305
Toll free: 1-800-461-2156
Fax: 807-343-7459

Website: www.ontario.ca/welcome-serviceontario

Prince Edward Island

Vital Statistics
126 Douses Road
Montague, PE C0A 1R0

Telephone: 902-838-0880
Toll free: 1-877-320-1253
Fax: 902-838-0883

Website: www.gov.pe.ca/vitalstatistics

Québec

Le Directeur de l'état civil
2535, boulevard Laurier
Québec, QC G1V 5C5

Telephone: 418-644-4545 or 514-644-4545
Toll free: 1-877-644-4545

Website: www.etatcivil.gouv.qc.ca/en/default.html
www.etatcivil.gouv.qc.ca/en/change-name.html

Email: etatcivil@dec.gouv.gc.ca

Saskatchewan

eHealth Saskatchewan
Vital Statistics Registry
2130 11th Avenue
Regina, SK S4P 0J5

Toll free: 855-347-5465

Fax: 306-787-2288

Email: VitalStatistics@ehealthsask.ca

Website:
www.ehealthsask.ca/vitalstats/Pages/default.aspx

Yukon

Vital Statistics
Box 2703
Whitehorse, YK Y1A 2C6

Couriers and Walk-ins: 4th floor–204 Lambert Street
Whitehorse, YK Y1A 3T2

Telephone: 867-667-5207
Toll free: 1-800-661-0408 (extension: 5207)
Fax: 867-393-6486

Email: Vital.Statistics@gov.yk.ca

Website: www.hss.gov.yk.ca/vitalstats.php

Offices Outside of Canada

United States

Contact the Vital Statistics office in the capital city of the state where the event occurred.

Website: www.cdc.gov/nchs/w2w.htm

England and Wales

Website: www.gro.gov.uk/gro/content/certificates

Scotland

Website: www.gro-scotland.gov.uk

Northern Ireland

Website:
www.nidirect.gov.uk/index/information-and-services/
government-citizens-and-rights/births-and-registration/
recording-change-of-name.htm

Other Countries

Contact the appropriate consulate to find out how to get the certificates you need.

Children Born Abroad to Armed Forces Personnel

National Defence and the Canadian Armed Forces
101 Colonel By Drive
Ottawa, ON K1A OK2

Telephone: 1-888-995-2534

Website: www.forces.gc.ca

Children Born Abroad to Canadian Parents

Contact the department of Citizenship and Immigration Canada:

Website: www.cic.gc.ca/english/citizenship/index.asp

Name Change Acts

Alberta

Contact Service Alberta if you would like a copy of the *Change of Name Act*; at time of printing the current version was not available online.

British Columbia

Name Act

www.bclaws.ca/Recon/document/ID/freeside/
00_96328_01

Manitoba

The Change of Name Act

web2.gov.mb.ca/laws/statutes/ccsm/c050e.php

The Change of Name Amendment Act

web2.gov.mb.ca/bills/39-5/b030e.php

New Brunswick

Change of Name Act

laws.gnb.ca/en/showpdf/cs/C-2.001.pdf

Newfoundland and Labrador

Change of Name Act, 2009

www.assembly.nl.ca/legislation/sr/annualstatutes/ 2009/
c08-1.c09.htm

Northwest Territories

Change of Name Act

www.justice.gov.nt.ca/FamilyLaw/legislation.shtml

Nova Scotia

Change of Name Act

nslegislature.ca/legc/statutes/change.htm

Nunavut

Consolidation of *Change of Name Act*

canlii.org/en/nu/laws/stat/rsnwt-nu-1988-c-c-3/latest/
rsnwt-nu-1988-c-c-3.pdf

Ontario

Change of Name Act

www.e-laws.gov.on.ca/html/statutes/english/elaws_
statutes_90c07_e.htm

Prince Edward Island

Change of Name Act

www.gov.pe.ca/law/statutes/pdf/c-03_1.pdf

Québec

Civil Code of Québec

www2.publicationsduquebec.gouv.qc.ca/
dynamicSearch/telecharge.php?type=2&file=/CCQ_1991/
CCQ1991_A.html

Saskatchewan

The Change of Name Act, 1995

www.qp.gov.sk.ca/documents/English/Statutes/
Statutes/C6-1.pdf

Yukon

Change of Name Act

www.gov.yk.ca/legislation/acts/chna.pdf

Appendix II

Identification Update List

- ❏ Banks
- ❏ Cable company
- ❏ Canada Revenue Agency
- ❏ Catalogues, magazines, newspaper subscriptions
- ❏ Clients or business associates
- ❏ Clubs
- ❏ Credit card companies
- ❏ Daycares and schools
- ❏ Dentist
- ❏ Doctor
- ❏ Driver's licence
- ❏ Employer
- ❏ Family and friends
- ❏ Frequent flier and loyalty card programs
- ❏ Health-care providers and health insurance

- ❏ Home insurance
- ❏ Internet provider
- ❏ Investment and financial planners
- ❏ Library card
- ❏ Life insurance
- ❏ Passport
- ❏ Pensions and retirement plans
- ❏ Phone company
- ❏ Post office/postal boxes
- ❏ Social insurance number
- ❏ Union
- ❏ Utility companies
- ❏ Vehicle insurance and registration
- ❏ _____
- ❏ _____
- ❏ _____
- ❏ _____
- ❏ _____
- ❏ _____
- ❏ _____
- ❏ _____
- ❏ _____

Download Kit

Please enter the URL you see in the box below into your computer web browser to access and download the kit.

> **www.self-counsel.com/updates/changename/kit14.htm**

The kit includes:

1. Alberta: Request to Amend an Alberta Vital Statistics Registration
2. Alberta: Changing a Child's Name
3. Alberta: Changing a Spouse's or Partner's Name
4. Alberta: Applicant Information
5. Alberta: Previous Change of Name Details
6. Alberta: Publication Notice
7. Alberta: Affidavit
8. British Columbia: Statutory Declaration Re: Correction of Error or Omission in Birth Registration
9. British Columbia: Application for Change of Name